MW01515210

Presented by: _____

From: _____

To: <u>Brenda</u>

God bless you!

Give God the Glory!

*Your Role in Your **Family***

By

Kevin Wayne Johnson

"Now the LORD had said unto Abram, Get thee out of thy country, and from thy kindred, and from thy father's house, unto a land that I will shew thee; And I will make of thee a great nation, and I will bless thee, and make thy name great; and thou shalt be a blessing: And I will bless them that Bless thee, and curse him that curseth thee: and in thee shall all families of the earth be blessed."

(Genesis 12: 1 – 3)

God's plan for the family is so important that He references *family* or *families* in *The Holy Bible* 285 times. Moreover, references to *father, mother,* and *child,* and their variations, are found 963, 325, and 1,957 times, respectively! In the first book of *The Holy Bible,* God reveals unto Abram *"...in thee shall all families of the earth be blessed* (Genesis 12:1-3)." So why has the world disregarded God's instructions pertaining to the family? I wanted to know why, so I studied, researched, prayed, observed, listened, read extensively, traveled, and wrote.

This is a companion and devotional book, to book #4 in the ***Give God the Glory***, book series. Devote time each day on this journey through the Scriptures to learn and understand *your* role in *your* family as God intends through His Word. It is specifically written with you in mind to reinforce the importance of the family institution. Let's explore, together, what God's plan was, and still is, for *His* family.

Now, let's ***Give God the Glory...***

Contents

1.

The Role and Purpose of the Godly Family

F-A-M-I-L-Y is mentioned 123 times in *The Holy Bible* – 122 in the Old Testament and once in the New Testament. In its original form, in the Greek language – *patria* – it means "an ancestry, lineage, family or tribe." Another translation – *oikos* – means "a household, family, a dwelling, a house."

God's first commandment to man, with a promise, deals with the *family.* Holiness in *family life* is evident in the Apostle Paul's teaching to the saints and faithful brethren in Christ (Colossians 1:2). In this dynamic teaching, God's Word clearly reveals His plans, roles, and responsibilities for the family that He created.

- Wives - …submit yourselves unto your **own** husbands, **as it is fit in the Lord** (Colossians 3:18).
- Husbands - …love **your** wives, and be not bitter against them (Colossians 3:19).
- Children - …obey your parents in **all** things: for this is **well pleasing unto the Lord** (Colossians 3:20).
- Fathers - …provoke not your children to anger, lest they be discouraged (Colossians 3:21).

"And I will bless them that bless thee, and curse him that curseth thee: and in thee shall all families of the earth be blessed."

(Genesis 12:3)

God's covenant with Abraham, because of his obedience, ensures that eternal blessings will flow through the family unit. *All* is an inclusive term – that means you and I. This is God's plan for our lives.

"And thy seed shall be as the dust of the earth, and thou shalt spread abroad to the west, and to the east, and to the north, and to the south: and in thee and in thy seed shall all the families of the earth be blessed."

(Genesis 28:14)

God's plan to bless His family extends across all boundaries, territories, countries, and nations. The God of Abraham, Isaac, and Jacob shall preserve His family unit throughout all time.

"Wherefore they are no more twain, but one flesh. What therefore God hath joined together, let no man put asunder."

(Matthew 19:6)

Man cannot destroy nor dissolve God's plan for His family. Futile attempts to alter the plan of God, as taught by Jesus, will never prosper. The ordained institution of marriage is God's manifestation of His unique characteristic: Oneness.

"And he answered and said unto them. Have ye not read, that he which made them at the beginning. MADE THEM MALE AND FEMALE, and said, FOR THIS CAUSE SHALL A MAN LEAVE FATHER AND MOTHER, AND SHALL CLEAVE TO HIS WIFE: AND THEY TWAIN SHALL BE ONE FLESH?"

(Matthew 19:4-5)

Unity within the family is characteristic of God's divine nature. One God, manifested three ways – Heavenly Father, Jesus Christ, and the Holy Spirit. God desires His family to be on one accord.

"And Adam said, This is now bone of my bones, and flesh of my flesh; she shall be called Woman, because she was taken out of Man."

(Genesis 2:23)

God created man and woman to reflect His image in creation and to complete each other (1 Corinthians 11:11-12). This is why God teaches us to love one another. The man that loves his wife also loves himself (Ephesians 5:28).

2.

The Role and Purpose of Man

God created man in *His* image, after *His* likeness, and game him (man) dominion over all the earth (Genesis 1:26). He did not stop there. God inspected all that He had made and declared it was *very good* (Genesis 1:31). Throughout *The Holy Bible*, there are over nine hundred references to *father* and four other variations. *Father*, a noun, derives from the Greek word – *patēr* – meaning "a nourisher, protector, and upholder." This word, in its singular form, is used 963 times. Other forms of this word include:

- fathers – 522 times,
- father's – 146 times,
- fathers' – 10 times, and
- fatherless – 41 times.

"And God said, Let us make man in our image, after our likeness: and let them have dominion over the fish of the sea, and over the fowl of the air; and over the cattle, and over all the earth, and over every creeping thing that creepeth upon the earth. So God created man in his own image in the image of God created he him; male and female created he them."

(Genesis 1:26-27)

God created man after Himself. Ultimately, man strives to emulate his Heavenly Father by patterning his lifestyle subject to God's character, conduct, commitment, consistency, and love. God is love (1 John 4:7-8) and the two cannot be separated.

"But I would have you know, that the head of every man is Christ; and the head of the woman is the man; and the head of Christ is God."

(1 Corinthians 11:3)

A man is called by God to treat his wife in the same manner that Jesus Christ would treat the church - honor, respect, and love. Ultimately, the woman should follow her husband as he follows Christ.

"Even every one that is called by my name: for I have created him for my glory, I have formed him; yea, I have made him."

(Isaiah 43:7)

The glory of God is personified by man as a means of expressing thanks to Him that created and formed us. Man is God's apex of creation. In return, men can choose to honor our Heavenly Father and teach our families to do the same.

"Thou art worthy, O Lord, to receive glory and honor and power: for thou hast created all things, and for thy pleasure they are and were created."

(Revelation 4:11)

John's vision into heaven reemphasizes that man was created for the glory of God. 'Glory' is mentioned 395 times throughout *The Holy Bible*. Since our Heavenly Father did create *all* things, He is definitely worthy to receive *all* glory and honor in our lives.

"...for in the image of God made he man."

(Genesis 9:6b)

'Image' is synonymous with *likeness* (Genesis
1:26 and 2 Corinthians 3:18). God created us to be
like our Heavenly Father – to think, feel, and decide.
Jesus Christ is the perfect image of God (2
Corinthians 4:4), and God is molding us back into
that perfect image (Romans 8:28-30).

"I will praise thee; for I am fearfully and wonderfully made: marvelous are thy works; and that my soul knoweth right well. My substance was not hid from thee when I was made in secret, and curiously wrought in the lowest parts of the earth. Thine eyes did see my substance, yet being unperfect; and in thy book all my members were written, which in continuance were fashioned, when as yet there was none of them."

(Psalms 139:14-16)

God know us intimately! The initial work of God is for us to believe in Jesus Christ. Apart from entering into this vital relationship, man cannot even begin to work for God. Psalm 139 is perhaps the most compassionate Scripture in *The Holy Bible* as it instructs the family man to know God, to know himself, and to know how to relate to others. These three key teachings are the essence of the Scriptures.

"Lo, this only have I found, that God hath made man upright; but they have sought out many inventions."

(Ecclesiastes 7:29)

There is strength in wisdom for the family man. Through the words of Solomon, he gives instruction warning about the futile emptiness of trying to be happy apart from God. 'Vanity' is a word that is used thirty-seven times to express the many things about life that cannot be understood: The futility of power, popularity, prestige, and pleasure apart from God. However, through wisdom, man can stand upright before his family and reveal that Jesus is Lord. They will follow.

"And the LORD God formed man of the dust of the ground, and breathed into his nostrils the breath of life; and man became a living soul."

(Genesis 2:7)

God is our source. Without Him, we are nothing. Man was formed out of the ground. It was not until God breathed into man the breath of life, that he became a living soul. As we look to our source for all things, He can and will grant us the desires of our heart. Man, then, becomes responsible to ensure that his family understands that God is indeed our source.

"And have put on the new man, which is renewed in knowledge after the image of him that created him."

(Colossians 3:10)

The Apostle Paul teaches the saints at Colosse that the position of the believer is to disregard their old ways and to saturate themselves into the kingdom of His (our Heavenly Father) dear Son (1:13). Knowledge and understanding of God's Word begins with a reverent fear of the Lord (Proverbs 1:7). Through this knowledge, man can teach his family to love God and to obey His commandments.

"A good man obtaineth favor of the LORD: but a man of wicked devices will he condemn."

(Proverbs 12:2)

God has designed His kingdom to acknowledge man's goodness toward Him and His Word. A key reward of choosing to love God and to acknowledge His will for our lives is that He will grant us favor in the earth.

3.

The Role and Purpose of Woman

The impact and role of the mother is so significant, thought-provoking, and meaningful to God, that He references *"mother,"* and its variations, in *The Holy Bible*, 325 times.

- Mother – 244 times,
- Mother's – 73 times,
- Mothers – 7 times, and
- Mothers' – once.

Further, *The Holy Bible* is much more descriptive of a godly woman in the book of Proverbs, chapter thirty-one, verses ten through thirty-one, than it is relative to a godly man and children. This concentrated passage of Scripture describes, in detail, the godly attributes of a wise woman as being happy, resourceful, strong, busy, influential, and endearing.

God created the woman to be a response mechanism. As a woman, and a mother in particular, you are designed to *respond* to a need. A woman is also fit, adaptable, and flexible. Thus, the *help meet* description of a woman (Genesis 2:18) characterizes her as fit and adaptable for man and for her role/purpose in the earth.

Genesis 2:18-25 fills in the details of the simple statement in Genesis 1:27, "...*male and female created He them.*" This account particularly amplifies the "and female" part of the statement and shows how woman was created.

"Who can find a virtuous woman? For her price is far above rubies."

(Proverbs 31:10)

'Virtuous' is defined and *conforming to moral and ethical principles, morally excellent, and upright.* A woman is so valuable in the sight of God that her price is far above the world's rarest stone – the ruby. A virtuous woman is also a crown to her husband (12:4).

"For a man indeed ought not to cover his head, forasmuch as he is the image and glory of God: but the woman is the glory of the man. For the man is not of the woman; but the woman for the man. Neither was the man created for the woman; but the woman for the man."

(1 Corinthians 11:7-9)

God predestined the order of His creation. His divine order is intended to simplify our lives and for us to clearly understand how God operates in the earth. 'Glory' in this context refers to the woman as a divine quality within her household. Her brightness, splendor, and radiance are an expression of God's presence in her life. In essence, she represents her husband as her husband represents Christ as His ambassador.

"A virtuous woman is a crown to her husband: but she that maketh ashamed is as rottenness in his bones."

(Proverbs 12:4)

Make your man proud! Represent him with honor and dignity. Do not deliberately bring shame to his name, character, or reputation. Represent Christ together in love and in unity as God intends.

"Therefore many of them believed: also of honorable women which were Greeks and of men, not a few."

(Acts 17:12)

Berea was a city in southern Macedonia. The Berean's set a good example as they willingly listened to preaching, but they checked the preaching against the Scriptures (verse 11). Amongst the many that received the preaching of Paul and Silas were honorable women. In the text, women are clearly lifted up as noble and honorable for obeying God's Word for their lives.

"For after this manner in the old time the holy women also, who trusted in God, adorned themselves, being in subjection unto their own husbands."

(1 Peter 3:5)

Love your husbands as they love you. Trust God and keep yourselves holy before Him. Respect your husbands' goals, vision, and God's will for his life, as he respects yours'. Grow in the Lord together and submit to one another at all times.

"Then cried a wise woman out of the city, Hear, hear; say, I pray you, unto Joab, Come near hither, that I may speak with thee."

(2 Samuel 20:16)

A wise woman is one who applies knowledge to real life, understands, and decides skillfully (Proverbs 10:5). The truly wise obey God. In this passage of Scripture, "a wise woman" imparted wisdom to Joab, nephew of King David, with cruel tendencies, that spared him from death by the hands of Sheba. Joab, though a king, had no prior knowledge that Sheba had conspired to kill him.

4.

The Role and Purpose of Children

The central reason for marriage is to provide children with mothers and fathers in a safe and loving environment. That said, children have two primary responsibilities in life: Obey their parents *in the Lord* while they are young, and honor and cherish their parents later in life, for the remainder of their lives.

Simply put, children are a gift from God! The references in *The Holy Bible* to child(ren) are close to 2,000 times as follows:

- Child – 198 times,
- Child's – 4 times,
- Children – 1,735 times,
- Children's – 18 times, and
- Childhood – twice.

Both the Old and New Testaments agree that children have only one responsibility in the family – to obey their parents. The admonition of Solomon is more fully explained by the Apostle Paul in the Book of Ephesians

6:1-3: *"Children, obey your parents in the Lord, for this is right. Honour thy father and mother; which is the first commandment with promise; That it may be well with thee, and thou mayest live long on the earth."*

Children is an inclusive term. It is not a matter of either sex or age that is involved. *Obey* has two meanings in its original Greek form:

> a. *hupakoē* (noun) – "Obedience and/or of the fulfillment of God's claims or commands."
>
> b. *Hupakouō* (verb) – "To listen, to attend." "To submit, to obey."

It is a profound word that is found 69 times in *The Holy Bible* and other variations of the word obey include obeyed, obeyedst, obeyeth, and obeying.

God's will for children is that they obey their parents. Two things are promised to children who obey their parents: (1) It will be well with them for they will have a happy life; and (2) They will have a long life. These are the two things that children want most and obedience to parents is the only way to assume them. That is why this is the first commandment with promise. From it springs all of the other important issues of life. The child who has not learned to obey his parents, who are God's representatives in the family, will not learn to obey God.

"Honour" is mentioned 142 times in *The Holy Bible*. Other variations of this word include:

- Honourable – 30 times,
- Honoured – 10 times,
- Honourest – Once,
- Honoureth – 8 times, and
- Honours – Once.

In its original Greek form – *timē* – it is a noun that means "a valuing." In order forms, it means glory – *doxa*. As a verb, it means "to honor" – *timaō*. Similarly, in its original Hebrew dialect – *kābēd* – honour means "to honor." This verb is used 114 times and in all periods of biblical Hebrew.

"Children, obey your parents in the Lord: for this is right. HONOR THY FATHER AND MOTHER; which is the first commandment with promise; THAT IT MAY BE WELL WITH THEE, AND THOU MAYEST LIVE LONG ON THE EARTH. And, ye fathers, provoke not your children to wrath: but bring them up in the nurture and admonition of the Lord."

(Ephesians 6:1-4)

A child has two primary responsibilities. First, to obey their Godly parents. Second, to honor them. This is the right thing to do. In return, God promises their wellness and a long life in the earth.

*"Verily I say unto you. Whosoever shall not receive
the kingdom of God as a little child
he shall not enter therein."*

(Mark 10:15)

A child represents innocence and open-mindedness. Through our open minds concerning God's will for our lives, He can transform our minds so that we can truly come to understand His kingdom.

"As newborn babes, desire the sincere milk of the word, that ye may grow thereby."

(1 Peter 2:2)

A thirst for God, and His will for our lives, can be quenched through His Word. The spiritual nourishment that it will provide will cause growth and development that will last forever. Then, as we grow in the Lord, pass it on to others within our sphere of influence through words, thoughts, and deeds.

"Brethren, be not children in understanding: howbeit in malice by ye children, but in understanding be men."

(1 Corinthians 14:20)

Children use their formative years to learn, grown, mature, and develop into Godly men and women. However, at a certain age, they must launch into an understanding of God's plan for our lives. Application of God's Word will produce fruit and strengthen our resolve to please God through our understanding of His commandments.

"The Spirit itself beareth witness with our spirit, that we are the children of God. And if children, then heirs; heirs of God, and joint-heirs with Christ; if so be that we suffer with him, that we may be also glorified together."

(Romans 8:16-17)

Our Heavenly Father reminds us daily that we are His children. As His children, He has left an inheritance – a right to have a personal relationship with Him through Jesus Christ – for us to enjoy. Hence, God is the father of all who believe in Christ in a special sense not shared by unbelievers. When we believe in Christ as Saviour, our estate is wonderfully changed from grim condemnation to privileged sonship.

"For ye were sometimes darkness, but now are ye light in the Lord: walk as children of light."

(Ephesians 5:8)

Light has divine qualities that include its radiance, penetrating force, it leads the way and guides, it dispels darkness, it exposes evil, and does not allow dark to occupy the same space(s). The Apostle Paul encouraged the believers at Ephesus to "walk as children of light." We used to walk in darkness before we established a relationship with God, through Jesus Christ. Now that we know better, walk upright before the Lord in everything that we do to bring Him glory.

"And he lifted up his eyes, and saw the women and the children; and said, Who are those with thee? And he said, The children which God hath graciously given thy servant."

(Genesis 33:5)

Children can be leaders given the appropriate circumstances. They were instrumental as servants who assisted Jacob to make peace with Esau. Do not underestimate their importance to the overall plan of God in our, and their, lives.

*"Furthermore we have had fathers of our flesh
which corrected us, and we gave them reverence:
shall we not much rather be in subjection
unto the Father of spirits and live?"*

(Hebrews 12:9)

Correction is pivotal in the life of a child. To withhold it is failure to demonstrate the principle of authority in their lives. As adults, we too must be subject to correction by our Heavenly Father. Corrective action is an act of love.

"Lo, children are a heritage of the LORD: and the fruit of the womb is his reward. As arrows are in the hand of a mighty man; so are children of the youth. Happy is the man that hath his quiver full of them: they shall not be ashamed but they shall speak with the enemies in the gate."

(Psalms 127:3-5)

Heritage is what we receive from our parents or ancestors. In this instance, our Heavenly Father's spiritual heritage are our children that He gives to us to raise in the nurture and admonition of the Lord. Our responsibility for these gifts from above are good stewardship and Godly oversight.

5.

God's Plan for His Family

The first-ever rating of prime television's portrayal of fatherhood was in 1999. It concluded that few fathers are to be found on prime-time television and those that are, usually are portrayed as incompetent or detached. Of the 102 shows originally reviewed only 15, or 14.7% featured a father who has children under the age of eighteen as a recurring central character. This study, conducted by the National Fatherhood Initiative, reviewed prime-time television on the five major networks from mid-November through mid-December, 1998.

With each generation, a myriad of facts reveal the deterioration of the family unit. Its current state is in a crisis mode, but has society considered what God has to say about it? A Supreme Court decision on January 22, 1973 – *Roe vs. Wade* – is partly attributable to the more than 40 million abortions performed in America since that time. That decision ruled that the right to personal property *includes* abortion. The USA Today newspaper ran a cover story on the front page on May 2, 2005 titled, *"The Changing Politics of Abortion."* The essence of the story centered on how political leaders voted relative to abortion rights – Is it or is it not legal to abort a child? Up to forty-five percent of Republican lawmakers polled agree that abortion is legal in a few circumstances. However, the middle verse of

The Holy Bible states, *"It is better to trust in the LORD than to put confidence in man"* (Psalms 118:8).

"For I know him, that he will command his children and his household after him, and they shall keep the way of the LORD, to do justice and judgment; that the LORD may bring upon Abraham that which he hath spoken of him."

(Genesis 18:19)

God trusted Abraham to the extent that he knew that his family would follow him in response to the assignment that Abraham was given. He knew that they would keep His commandments and that all families of the earth would be blessed after him. It was because of Abraham's faith that God lifted him up as an awesome leader of men. Many generations later, we still feel the impact of the manifold family blessings because of Abraham's faith in God.

"And God blessed them, and God said unto them, Be fruitful, and multiply, and replenish the earth, and subdue it: and have dominion over the fish of the sea, and over the fowl of the air, and over every living thing that moveth upon the earth."

(Genesis 1:28)

God's mandate for us all is to be productive according to God's will for our lives, raise the level of productivity of those within our sphere of influence, leave a deposit in the earth for the next generation, and to control our environment.

"Honour thy father and thy mother: that thy days may be long upon the land which the LORD thy God giveth thee."

(Exodus 20:12)

This is one of the original Ten Commandments, from God to man, that relates specifically to man. It admonishes children to honor their parents so that God may prolong their lives. It is mentioned again in Ephesians 6:2.

"Then he said, I pray thee therefore, father, that thou wouldest send him to my father's house: for I have five brethen, that he may testify unto them, lest they also come into this place of torment."

(Luke 16:27-28)

In this parable, Jesus teaches a powerful message about common concern within the family. "The rich man's" torment is so great, that he desires to warn his five brothers. This concern for his siblings reflects love within the family unit. Although he cannot save himself, perhaps he can warn others to stay away from their evil ways that lead to eternal torment.

"Let the husband render unto the wife due benevolence: and likewise also the wife unto the husband."

(1 Corinthians 7:3)

Principles in marriage life include equal affection one to another. Chapter seven of this book of *The Holy Bible* teaches four key elements for the Godly family: Principles for married life, Abiding in God's call, Principles for the unmarried, and Principles for remarriage. Be kind, gentle, and affectionate toward each other. Demonstrate the kind of love that our Heavenly Father demonstrates toward us.

"When I call to remembrance the unfeigned faith that is in thee, which dwelt first in thy grandmother Lois, and thy mother Eunice; and I am persuaded that in thee also."

(2 Timothy 1:5)

Young Timothy grew up to become a pastor and was encouraged by the Apostle Paul to remember his maternal grandmother, and mother, for their role in his Godly maturity. One of the best things that we can leave for our children, and children's children, is a clear example of who God is. This is not only revealed by what we may know, but how we live our lives.

God's Plan for the Family

Simply put, *family* centers around mom and dad. It means:

Father

And

Mother

I

Love

You

God's first commandment, which is sealed with a promise, centers around the *family* and family life. This is revealed twice in the Old Testament *(Exodus 20:12* – one of the original Ten Commandments – and again in *Deuteronomy 5:16)*. The New Testament revelation is written as follows:

HONOUR THY FATHER AND MOTHER which is the **first commandment with promise.** *THAT IT MAY BE WELL WITH THEE. AND THOU MAYEST LIVE LONG ON THE EARTH.*
(Ephesians 6:2-3)

F-A-M-I-L-Y is mentioned 123 times in *The Holy Bible* – 122 in the Old Testament and once in the New Testament. In its original form, in the Greek language – *patria* – it means "an ancestry, lineage, family or tribe." Another translation – *oikos* – means "a household, family, a dwelling, a house."

Contact Kevin Wayne Johnson at:
Writing for the Lord Ministries
Clarksville, Maryland
www.writingforthelord.com
Kevin@writingforthelord.com

<u>Other books by Kevin Wayne Johnson</u>

Give God the Glory! – Series

Know God & Do the Will of God Concerning Your life ©
2001

Called to be Light in the Workplace © *2003*

Let Your Light So Shine © *2004*

The Godly Family Life © *2005*

To order more copies of this book, or other books,
contact:

Writing for the Lord Ministries

6400 Shannon Court
Clarksville, Maryland 21029
www.writingforthelord.com
(443) 535-0475 • (410) 340-8633

Writing for the Lord
M I N I S T R I E S

CPSIA information can be obtained at www.ICGtesting.com
Printed in the USA
BVOW021122130613

323047BV00009B/100/P